Summary of

Capital in the Twenty-First Century

by Thomas Piketty

Instaread

Please Note

This is a summary with analysis.

Table of Contents

Overview

Thomas Piketty's *Capital in the Twenty-First Century* is a study of inequity, both historically and in the present. The book describes how the concentration of wealth has changed over time. Its central thesis is that return on capital is greater than growth over time, which means that capital and inequality inevitably increase. The book also considers the ways governments might address the increasing concentration of wealth in the future.

Many economists have argued that increasing worker productivity in the modern era will inevitably result in reduced inequality. The historical record suggests that this is untrue. For most of history, there has been a huge gap between the rich and poor with no real middle class.

That changed in developed countries during the twentieth century for a number of reasons. First, two world wars caused massive shocks to the status quo and resulted in severe losses to many holders of capital. Second, to finance the wars, many governments quickly passed new progressive income taxes. These taxes changed the structure of wealth in society and created the possibility for a middle class of small capital holders.

Over time, in societies without strong growth, capital tends to concentrate and accumulate. This can be expressed as r>g. In this expression, r stands for the average rate of return on capital, and g stands for the rate of growth of the economy. Over time, return on capital tends to be higher than the growth of the economy. Thus capital accumulates faster than the economy can grow, which means capitalists become more and more wealthy in comparison to everyone else.

High growth rates during the nineteenth and twentieth centuries thus helped to create a more equal distribution of wealth. However, in the twenty-first century, growth has slowed. The world again is seeing high levels of inequality similar to those in the eighteenth and early nineteenth centuries. This inequality is likely to increase unless it is addressed.

The best way to halt or reverse rising inequality is through increased taxation. Especially in Britain and the United States, where top salaries, particularly for CEOs, have increased rapidly, a confiscatory tax on very high incomes would help to rein in excessive salary divergence.

A global tax on capital is the central tool governments need to control and manage inequality. Such a tax would first provide researchers and the public with essential records about who owns what capital worldwide. Policy decisions could then be much better informed. A global tax would also prevent individuals from relocating assets in order to avoid national tax authorities. Finally, such a tax would help fund governments, providing the where-withal to create safety nets, stabilize employment, and preserve the middle class while helping the poor.

Capital in the Twenty-First Century was published in 2013 in French. The English translation in 2014 became a #1 *New York Times* bestseller and an international sensation. Piketty's argument prompted an intense and ongoing dis-cussion of the nature and danger of inequality.

Important People

Thomas Piketty is a French economist who studies income and wealth inequality.

Arthur Goldhammer is senior affiliate at the Center for European Studies at Harvard and a renowned translator of French. He translated *Capital in the Twenty-First Century* into English.

Karl Marx (1818-1883) was a Prussian economist who advocated for Communist revolution. His most famous works include *The Communist Manifesto* (1848) and *Capital* (1867).

Simon Kuznets (1901-1985) was an American economist known for his work on economic growth and for his pioneering use of statistics and quantitative sources.

Jane Austen (1775-1817) was a British novelist.

Honoré de Balzac (1799-1850) was a French novelist.

Thomas Malthus (1766-1834) was an English economist who believed that unchecked population growth was dangerous and would lead inevitably to famine and disease.

David Ricardo (1772-1823) was a British economist known for his work on the theory of land rents.

Franco Modigliani (1918-2003) was a Nobel-prize winning Italian economist. He developed the life-cycle hypothesis, which theorizes that people save to ensure a stable level of consumption over their lifetimes.

Key Takeaways

1. Discussions of inequality are innately political. Economists who write about inequality are always influenced by their own political prejudices and preconceptions.

2. The capital/income ratio is an important indicator of inequality in a society.

3. When growth is low, the capital/income ratio is high, and societies tend to become more unequal.

4. There is no guarantee that inequality will lessen in the modern era. Rather, inequality decreased in the twentieth century because of specific events, such as the two World Wars, and specific policies, such as the progressive income tax.

5. The vast majority of wealth in the twenty-first century is private wealth. Governments can either borrow or tax private wealth. The wealthy much prefer government borrowing, but this does not necessarily benefit governments or others in society.

6. Despite increased life expectancy, inheritance continues to be of major importance in perpetuating wealth.

7. Inequality in the twenty-first century is different from that of earlier eras in that it is partially

fueled by massive income divergence. A confiscatory tax on very high incomes could help to address this problem.

8. A global tax on capital is needed to control inequality and prevent injustice and instability.

Thank you for purchasing this Instaread book

**Download the Instaread mobile app to get
unlimited text & audio summaries
of bestselling books.**

Visit Instaread.co
to learn more.

Analysis

Key Takeaway 1

Discussions of inequality are innately political. Economists who write about inequality are always influenced by their own political prejudices and preconceptions.

Analysis

Some economists present economics as a science that objectively describes financial conditions and provides technical guides to optimal policies. The truth, however, is that economic decisions are political ones, and economic theories have always been influenced by the political and social position of economists. For example, economists in modern Western societies in the twenty-first century tend to occupy respected positions of power and comfort. As a result, many such economists see the future in optimistic terms and are not overly worried about growing inequality.

One of the most glaring examples of the way in which politics and economics are intertwined is in the history of supply-side economics. Supply-side economics argues that lowering tax rates causes people to work harder and that this stimulates growth. Supply-side economics also holds that cutting taxes on the wealthy is particularly effective because tax cuts lead the wealthy to spend and invest more, causing a trickle-down effect throughout the economy. [1]

In the United States, supply-side economics is associated with the administration of Republican President Ronald Reagan. It remains a core platform for conservatives. The conservative Heritage Foundation, for example, has strongly supported supply-side tax cuts, arguing that they stimulate growth. [2] The liberal journal *Democracy*, on the other hand, points to numerous studies showing that supply-side tax cuts have had little effect on growth. [3]

As this division shows, supply-side arguments are not simply empirical. They are bound up with political goals. Conservatives prefer supply-side economics because they believe higher tax rates for the rich are unjust. In the United States, Republicans tend to be richer than Democrats, so it is in their self-interest to avoid taxes that would redistribute wealth to the poor. [4].

On the other hand, Democrats tend to be poorer, and Democratic politicians often support higher taxes in order to redistribute wealth and resources to those less well-off. The conservative think tank AEI points out that Democrats rarely discuss Democratic President John F. Kennedy's tax cuts and the subsequent decade of growth because cutting taxes does not fit with current Democratic priorities. [5] Economists use data, but how that data is used depends on political and personal considerations as the debate over supply-side economics demonstrates.

Key Takeaway 2

The capital/income ratio is an important indicator of inequality in a society.

Analysis

The capital/income ratio, represented by the Greek letter β, is the ratio of the total stock of capital to the annual flow of income per year. In societies with very high inequality, the capital/income ratio also tends to be high. In Europe in the 1800s and early 1900s, the amount of capital in each country was equal to about six or seven years of national income. In a society with such a high capital/income ratio, the country's money is super-concentrated in old capital, which dwarfs current productivity. In contrast, in Europe between the beginning of World War I in 1914 and the end of World War II in 1945, the capital/income ratio fell to two to three years of national income. This created a much more egalitarian society in which workers could generate wealth during their own lifetimes that rivaled inherited wealth.

To understand capital/income ratio, consider a pre-capitalist hunter-gatherer society. Friedrich Engels, Karl Marx's collaborator, considered these societies to be ideal in their equality; he described pre-capitalist social arrangements as "primitive communism." [6] Part of the reason that hunter-gatherer societies appealed to Engels and other Communists is that the capital/income ratio was very low or even effectively equal. People in such cultures have few possessions and little ability to store food or goods because they are constantly on the move. Individuals might accumulate some jewelry or engraved weapons, but even that would be limited to what they could carry. Capital, or stored wealth, would be at best only slightly greater than income, or the wealth gained through gathering and occasionally killing animals. Such a society would be more or less egalitarian; the richest person, with the most elaborate jewelry and goods, would still only be a little wealthier than the poorest, who could reasonably acquire just as much as the wealthiest with a few lucky kills or simply by saving or trading cannily.

In fact, anthropologists have found that small-scale hunter-gatherer societies were very egalitarian as might be expected by considering their capital/income ratio. However, even small, relatively equal societies need to work to prevent capital accumulation. Small-scale societies enforce equality through a number of norms and customs. Those who acquire too much power or capital are often mocked or insulted and may even be the target of violence. [7]

Key Takeaway 3

When growth is low, the capital/income ratio is high, and societies tend to become more unequal.

Analysis

Over the long run, β=savings/growth. In other words, the capital/income ratio is directly related to the amount of savings. The more savings there are, the greater the capital/income ratio will be.

In contrast, β is inversely related to growth. This means that when the capital/income ratio is low, growth will be high. In this situation, money acquired by work rivals capital already saved or invested. As a result, workers are better off relative to capitalists. When growth decreases, on the other hand, the rate of return on capital becomes greater than the growth of income and output. This quickly creates inequalities because those who control capital get higher returns on their wealth while those without capital fall further behind.

The predominance of capital over growth through much of history is illustrated in novels by Honoré de Balzac and Jane Austen. Even fairy tales describe the mechanisms of inequality. Cinderella, a story with variants all across Europe, is usually considered a fantasy. Cinderella is saved from a life of toil when her fairy godmother helps her attract the attention of a handsome, wealthy prince. The magic elements in the tale, however, rest upon an economic reality. In most periods, and certainly in the medieval era when Cinderella is set, earnings from capital far outstripped growth rates. Wealthy property owners like Prince Charming did not need to work; they were free to cultivate charming and leisurely pursuits. The simple fact of Cinderella's orphanhood quickly demoted her social standing to that a servant girl, signaling the precarity of women's economic lives, as it was difficult for them to inherit property. Instead, marrying wealth was often the only way for someone like Cinderella, who lacked economic opportunity, to escape a life of drudgery. The fairy tale may seem unrealistic, but it accurately reflects the difficulties of social mobility in a society where capital heavily outweighs growth.

Key Takeaway 4

There is no guarantee that inequality will lessen in the modern era. Rather, inequality decreased in the twentieth century because of specific events, such as the two World Wars, and specific policies, such as the progressive income tax.

Analysis

Many economists have argued that society will naturally progress towards greater equality as education improves and more people have better skills with which to earn higher incomes. In practice, however, the historical record does not show steady progress towards equality. Rather, it shows a long period of inequality before the twentieth century. Then, World War I and World War II caused great dislocations in capital as wealthy Europeans lost ownership of colonies and upheavals destroyed property and wealth.

Many nations passed progressive income taxes to fund the war effort, which redistributed capital and wealth. It was this redistribution that made possible a substantial middle class. After the shocks of the wars, however, inequality began to grow again and continues to do so.

It was not just World War I and World War II that reduced wealth inequality; wars in general can have a redistributive effect. This was the case during the Civil War. The wealthiest Southerners lost large amounts of what was considered their property when the slaves were freed. In addition, plantations were damaged during the war. As a result, during the 1860s, wealth inequalities dropped in the South. [8]

This process is famously dramatized in Margaret Mitchell's 1936 novel *Gone With the Wind*. In that novel, the society before the war is similar to the France described by Honoré de Balzac in his novels. Scarlett O'Hara's suitors rely for their status and rank on the position of their family and inheritance. In nineteenth-century America, as in nineteenth-century France, capital mattered more than work as long as there was peace. But when war breaks out, Scarlett loses much of her wealth and is forced to abandon her life of leisure in order to earn a living as an industrialist. Through her connections and resources, however, Scarlett manages to stabilize her own financial position. Similarly, over time, the economic disruption caused by the Civil War stabilized. Inequality climbed again, until it had reached another peak by 1929. [9] Similarly, France following World War II has moved back in the direction of greater inequality. While dramatic events can promote equality, there is not necessarily any long-term trend towards more equal wealth distribution.

Key Takeaway 5

The vast majority of wealth in the twenty-first century is private wealth. Governments can either borrow or tax private wealth. The wealthy much prefer government borrowing, but this does not necessarily benefit governments or others in society.

Analysis

In most developed countries, governments have little or even negative public wealth. Governments own many assets including buildings, land, equipment, and patents. However, they also have large debts, which cancel out their assets. This means that the vast majority of wealth in developed nations is private. In order to finance government services, therefore, governments must tap private wealth through taxation or borrowing.

The wealthy generally prefer that the government borrow from them rather than take their money through taxation. When people lend to the government, they receive interest payments; they get to charge for the use of their money. A tax means that the wealthy must simply hand over money with no return.

The wealthy dislike this. But taxation enables government to provide services without contracting debts. Financing government through borrowing, on the other hand, can lead to greater inequality because the government is paying out considerable sums to those who already have significant private wealth.

The French have the highest tax rates in Europe, higher even than notoriously high-tax Sweden. In 2012, a socialist president, François Hollande, was elected with a promise to raise rates to 75 percent on the very wealthy. These rates may seem burdensome, but the French see them as acceptable because they subsidize social services, such as good hospitals, free daycare, and efficient public transportation. If France were paying for the use of rich people's money by borrowing it rather than confiscating it through taxation, there would be less to go around for social services, which would ultimately mean a lower standard of living for the poor and greater inequality. [10]

As in the United States, the wealthy in France often resent such high taxes. Film star Gerard Depardieu left France in 2012 to avoid the tax burden. [11] The fact that the rich can avoid taxes is one incentive for governments to borrow instead—and is also why international tax agreements could help all nations stabilize their revenue and finances.

Key Takeaway 6

Despite increased life expectancy, inheritance continues to be of major importance in perpetuating wealth.

Analysis

It is true that long life spans have delayed the moment at which heirs receive money; as a result, even relatively well-off heirs tend to pursue careers. However, the late onset of inherited wealth is somewhat deceptive. While they are still alive, the wealthy often give their heirs gifts. The value of gifts has in fact been increasing; between 1870 and 1970, gifts amounted to around 20-30 percent of inherited wealth. In 2000-2010, gifts had climbed to 80 percent of inherited wealth.

Like other measures of inequality, the importance of inheritance dipped in the period after World War II. But it has been on the rise in the 2000s, and that trend is likely to continue. A 2015 Wealth-X and NFP Family Transfers Report demonstrates the ongoing importance of inheritance. The study found that between 2015 and 2045, people in the world with net worth of over $30 million would pass on $16 trillion in property, cash, and other wealth to their families. [12] A strong estate tax is required to put limits on the perpetuation of inequality from generation to generation and to ensure that the value of work does not dwindle into insignificance in comparison to the value of inheritance.

Key Takeaway 7

Inequality in the twenty-first century is different from that of earlier eras in that it is partially fueled by massive income divergence. A confiscatory tax on very high incomes could help to address this problem.

Analysis

In the 1800s, the richest people often didn't work at all; their income came entirely from capital and rents. Today, however, the wealthy are much more likely to work and, in many cases, have extremely high incomes. This is especially the case in the United States, where high CEO pay has become notorious.

The ballooning of top executive pay began under President Ronald Reagan in the 1980s. Before that time, the United States had pioneered the use of confiscatory tax rates to rein in excessive income and promote equality. Taxes on top earners could be over 70 percent. Following the slumping economy of the 1970s, conservatives argued that high taxes were stifling the economy. This argument won out, and Congress slashed top tax rates in the United States to around 40 percent. As a result, CEOs, who often control their own compensation packages, have no incentive to rein in their salaries.

One way to illustrate the growing income gap is to compare the pay of a CEO at a given firm to the median worker pay at the same firm. A 2015 report found that in the United States, CEOs are paid on average 204 times as much as the median worker in their firms. The report found that four CEOs earned fully a thousand times as much as their median workers. CEO David Zaslav of Discovery Communication had the biggest pay inequity. He earned $156.1 million in 2014, which means his compensation was 1,951 times that of Discovery Communication's median worker, who earned $80,000. [13] This is a huge disparity in itself, but it looms even larger if one considers that the inequality is multiplied year over year. The median worker can save much less in each year than Zaslav. That means Zaslav's fortune will be thousands and thousands of times greater than the median worker's when he passes it on to his heirs. With their wealth, connections, and access to the best education, Zaslav's heirs in turn will be in a position to earn exorbitant salaries themselves.

Surging top incomes could potentially create a new kind of inequality in which those at the top have both huge reserves of capital and massive yearly incomes. Without intervention, this could mean more lopsided inequality than the levels seen in the eighteenth or early nineteenth centuries.

Key Takeaway 8

A global tax on capital is needed to control inequality and prevent injustice and instability.

Analysis

Growing inequality can corrupt political systems because individuals with massive wealth can influence politicians in unjust ways. Inequality also creates resentment, exacerbates poverty, and can lead to political anger, frustration, and violence.

A capital tax on all wealth would be the ideal way to help counteract the tendency of capital and wealth to accumulate. Even a small tax would be useful because it would force the wealthy to disclose their assets. At present, there are no good, comprehensive records of the distribution of wealth. It is difficult to make policy when the extent of inequality is unknown. Even a nominal tax on capital, therefore, could have enormous benefits in making global inequalities transparent and comprehensible.

A global tax is probably utopian. But regional taxes would be a step in the right direction. Countries, especially in Europe, are afraid to tax capital because they worry that businesses or individuals will simply move across the border if they are taxed. A European Union capital tax could be a first step towards more global agreements.

The importance of a global tax was emphasized in 2016 with the release of the Panama Papers, leaked documents from a Panamanian law firm, Mossack Fonseca. The Panama Papers show how the firm has been helping wealthy and politically powerful people create companies to hold their assets. The companies hide the real ownership of the assets and thereby deceive tax collectors. [14]

The tax shelters have been used by wealthy people throughout the world including politicians in Russia and in Iceland and have caused scandals. The Panama Papers also show that the wealthy routinely fail to pay their taxes. In fact, the best estimates suggest that there are $7.6 trillion in offshore tax havens worldwide, which is around 8 percent of the world's wealth. Taxing that money could help governments provide services for the poor and middle classes. Instead, the money simply accumulates in offshore bank accounts, making the powerful even more so. A global tax on capital, or at the very least better global coordination to deter tax evasion, is desperately needed to address these injustices. [15]

Author's Style

Capital in the Twenty-First Century has sold more than 2 million copies as of early 2016. [16] The book's success was a surprise, and it was not necessarily intended for a vast audience. Still, it's not hard to see why it had success. Piketty uses concrete examples to make his points. In particular, he draws ideas and illustrations from the novels of Jane Austen and Honoré de Balzac. These parts of the book are entertaining and help clarify his argument. Piketty also has a dry humor which surfaces now and then and helps make the book a bit more entertaining.

Many sections are less lively, however. As academics are wont to do, Piketty spends a lot of time distinguishing his position from that of other economists. He also uses math and equations with some frequency. While he takes care to explain his concepts for general readers, the technical details can become cumbersome at times. His prose, while clear, is not pithy; his sentences are long and his vocabulary is academic.

Author's Perspective

As a French economist, Thomas Piketty is interested in France and in Europe more generally. Many of his historical examples are drawn from French data and the French experience. Similarly, he tends to focus on European problems and to offer solutions to Europe specifically, though his book also considers the United States and other regions of the world in depth.

Politically, Piketty endorses policies that would be considered left-leaning in the United States—he argues for higher taxes on income, estates, and wealth. His conclusions are based in part on his work and research. However, he does not present his suggested policies as objective solutions. Though he is an economist, Piketty feels strongly that economics is too important to be left to professionals. He argues that economics is not a science and that economists cannot arrive at objective, scientific answers to political questions. Rather, arguments about wealth and inequality must be settled through the political process and through legitimate elected institutions. Piketty studies inequality from the perspective of a person committed to democracy. This is why he thinks inequality is dangerous and why he is unwilling to impose a one-size-fits-all solution without referring to the will of the voters.

~~~~ END OF INSTAREAD ~~~~

Thank you for purchasing this Instaread book

**Download the Instaread mobile app to get
unlimited text & audio summaries
of bestselling books.**

Visit Instaread.co
to learn more.

References

1. Tanden, Neera. "Burying Supply-Side Once and for All." *Democracy: A Journal of Ideas*, Summer 2013, No. 29. Accessed April 12, 2016. http://democracyjournal.org/magazine/29/burying-supply-side-once-and-for-all/

2. Mitchell, Daniel J. "A 'Supply-Side' Success Story." Heritage Foundation, June 7, 2005. Accessed April 12, 2016. http://www.heritage.org/research/reports/2005/06/a-supply-side-success-story

3. Tanden.

4. Gelman, Andrew. "Richer people continue to vote Republican." *The Monkey Cage*, November 14, 2012. Accessed April 12, 2016. http://themonkeycage.org/2012/11/richer-people-continue-to-vote-republican/

5. Perry, Mark J. "Let's not forget the decade liberals love to hate: The 1960s and President Kennedy's successful, supply-side tax cuts." *AEI*, August 17, 2013. Accessed May 13, 2016. http://www.aei.org/publication/lets-not-forget-the-decade-the-liberals-love-to-hate-the-1960s-and-president-kennedys-successful-supply-side-tax-cuts/

6. Empson, Martin. "Primitive communism: life before class and oppression." *Socialist*

Worker, May 28, 2013. Accessed May 16, 2016. https://socialistworker.co.uk/art/33429/Primitive+communism%3A+life+before+class+and+oppression

7. Turchin, Peter. "The Z-Curve of Human Egalitarianism." *Social Evolution Forum*, April 16, 2012. Accessed April 13, 2016. https://evolution-institute.org/blog/the-z-curve-of-human-egalitarianism/

8. Skidmore, Felicity. "Long-Term Trends in American Wealth Inequality." *Focus*, 3:1, 1978. Accessed April 14, 2016. http://www.irp.wisc.edu/publications/focus/pdfs/foc31c.pdf

9. Ibid.

10. *Economist*. "Why do the French tolerate such high taxes?" September 24, 2013. Accessed May 6, 2016. http://www.economist.com/blogs/economist-explains/2013/09/economist-explains-13

11. Ibid.

12. *Wealth X*. "Family Wealth Transfers Report." January 2015, pp. 6-7. Accessed May 10, 2016. http://www.wealthx.com/wp-content/uploads/2015/01/WealthX_NFP_FamilyWealthTransfersReport-2014.pdf

13. Che, Jenny. "Here's How Outrageous The Pay Gap Between CEOs And Workers Is." *Huffington Post*, August 27, 2015. Accessed April 15, 2016. http://www.huffingtonpost.com/entry/ceo-worker-pay-gap_us_55ddc3c7e-4b0a40aa3acd1c9

14. Yglesias, Matthew. "Panama Papers: a massive document leak reveals a global web of corruption and tax avoidance." *Vox*, April 3, 2016. Accessed April 15, 2016. http://www.vox.com/2016/4/3/11356326/panama-papers

15. Ibid.

16. Rowlatt, Justin. "Thomas Piketty: 'Indian inequality still hidden.'" BBC News, May 2, 2016. Accessed May 6, 2016. http://www.bbc.com/news/world-asia-india-36186116

CPSIA information can be obtained
at www.ICGtesting.com
Printed in the USA
LVHW02s1441200818
587523LV00014B/831/P